Photo: Keith Saunders

VANESSA BATES writes for theatre, television, film and radio. Plays include *Darling Oscar*, *Checklist For An Armed Robber*, *Hunger, Match*, *Every Second*, *Lakes of Death & Dreamers*, *A Little Bit Each Night* and *The Elephant's Ark*. She has been produced by the Sydney Theatre Company, Griffin Theatre, Vitalstatistix, Theatre@Risk, Deckchair Theatre, Belvoir B-Sharp, Tantrum Theatre and ABC Radio. Her work has been shortlisted for the Victorian Premier's Literary Award and the Patrick White Playwright Award and won an AWGIE and two Inscriptions Awards. Vanessa is a NIDA Playwright's Studio graduate and one seventh of playwrights' alliance 7-ON.

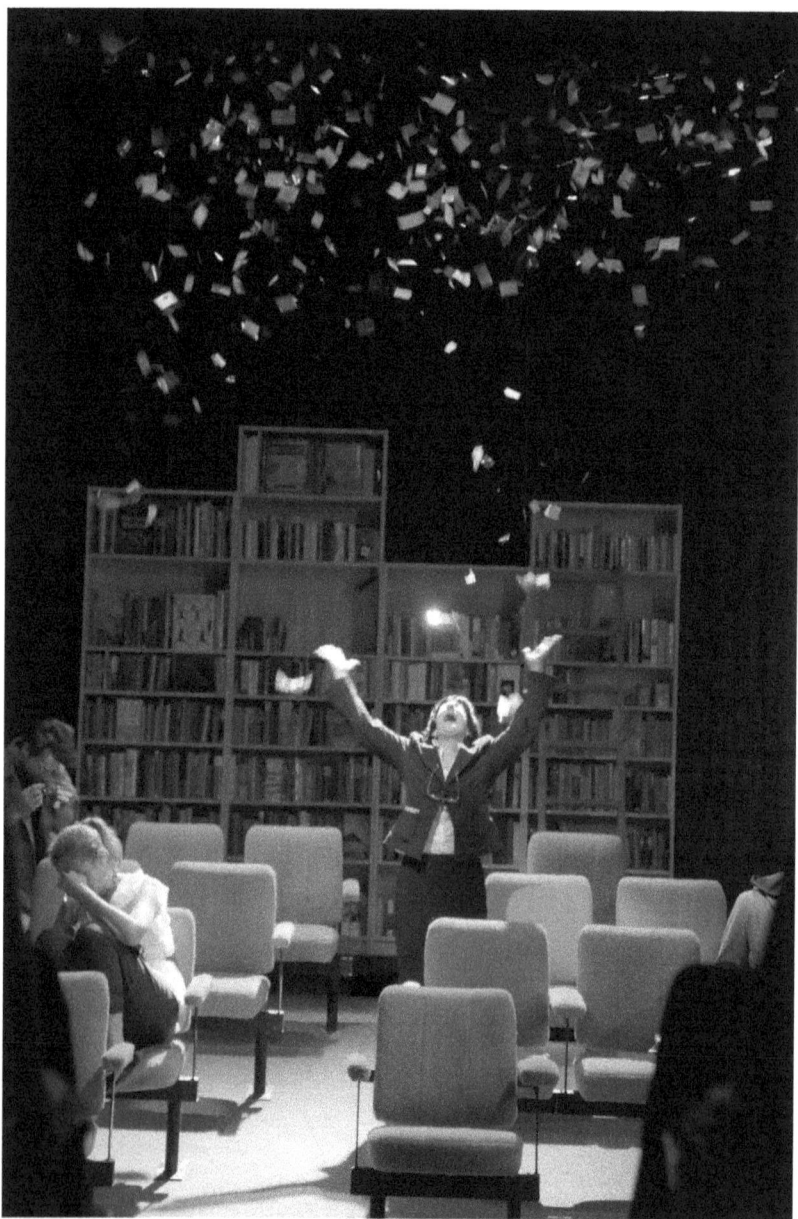

Brendan Hanson, Caitlin Beresford-Ord, Vivienne Garrett and Tim Solly (partially obscured) in the 2009 Deckchair Theatre production. (Photo: Nick Merrylees)

CHECKLIST
FOR AN
ARMED ROBBER

VANESSA BATES

Currency Press, Sydney

CURRENCY PLAYS

First published in 2009
by Currency Press Pty Ltd,
PO Box 2287, Strawberry Hills, NSW, 2012, Australia
enquiries@currency.com.au
www.currency.com.au

NATIONAL LIBRARY OF AUSTRALIA CIP DATA

Author:	Bates, Vanessa.
Title:	Checklist for an armed robber / Vanessa Bates.
ISBN:	9780868198637 (pbk.)
Dewey Number:	A822.4

Typeset by Dean Nottle for Currency Press.
Cover design by Emma Vine, Currency Press.
Front cover shows Paul Ashcroft. Back cover shows Ryan Gibson, Edwina Wren,
Natalia Novikova, Paul Ashcroft. Photography by Josephine Harkin.

Currency Press acknowledges the Traditional Owners of the Country on which
we live and work. We pay our respects to all Aboriginal and Torres Strait
Islander Elders, past and present.

Contents

Australian Government

Australia Council
for the Arts

Publication of this title was assisted by
the Commonwealth Government through
the Australia Council, its arts funding and
advisory body.

ACKNOWLEDGEMENTS

Checklist for an Armed Robber was written as part of the Sydney Theatre Company's Blueprints Literary Program in 2003/4. Thanks to the original workshop and improvisation cast: Jeanette Cronin, Tim Richards, Paul Barry and Tanya Goldberg and director Melinda Collie-Holmes. Thanks also to Blueprints Literary Program director Nick Marchand.

And to Todd for telling us the secret and more.

The two articles used as springboard for Checklist for an Armed Robber were: 'Robber is offered a banana but settles for two books' by Frances O'Shea, published in the Daily Telegraph on 31 October 2002 and 'I tried and failed' by Anna Politkovskaya and published in The Guardian on 30 October 2002.

Behind the Headlines

Chris Bendall

I first read Vanessa Bates' startling *Checklist for an Armed Robber* in mid-2006, and was immediately struck by the play's innovative and original form. Here was a work so assured in its craft, and so inspired in its use of theatrical form, and perhaps most significantly so *gripping*, that I immediately wanted to direct it. I had already encountered Bates' unique theatrical voice in an earlier, highly entertaining work called *Darling Oscar*, and was keen to see her work produced in Melbourne.

Starting with newspaper reports of two events that took place on opposite ends of the globe over the same weekend, Bates has crafted a play that is rich in ideas, rich in language and that carries a powerful emotional punch. *Checklist for an Armed Robber* deftly interweaves the story of the 2002 siege of a Russian theatre in Moscow, and an attempted armed robbery of a new age bookstore in Newcastle, Australia. The juxtaposition of these two seemingly unconnected events creates an exhilarating, often poignant and frequently humorous exploration of fear, hope and compassion that is ultimately universal.

The central focus of Bates' play is an examination of the root causes of these acts of desperation and violence, rather than the acts themselves. This is not merely a play about terrorism or violence, but a work that looks behind the headlines, and explores the lives that lead up to such acts of desperation. We are faced every day with media reports sensationalising acts of violence and terror (which of course simply increases the reach of the terrorists aim—to inspire terror). But in this play, we are allowed what we so rarely have a chance to witness and hear—the voices of these same 'terrorists' expressing why they have ultimately taken this desperate and deadly solution to their crisis. By personalising these voices, we are forced to ask the very difficult question 'why?'.

Checklist For An Armed Robber explores the anonymous face of terrorism from the micro to the macro. The play examines the way terrorism impacts on the lives of the innocent, while simultaneously seeking to understand what motivates these acts. It questions how we find the courage and compassion needed to halt cycles of violence.

By counterpointing the preparations of a young man preparing to hold up a single shopkeeper against the struggles of a Chechen terrorist leader before and during an horrific extended siege, where several hundred innocent audience members were taken hostage for three days, Bates forces us to draw comparisons between the two events. The connection is far deeper than we first imagine. The most obvious similarity is time: the two events happened over the same weekend. Also, the two antagonists that Bates focuses on are both young men and central to both of the narratives is a negotiation between a younger man and an older woman (the bookseller in one instance, a journalist negotiating for the release of hostages in the other). But it is the discrepancies between the haves and the have nots that takes this work beyond mere surface connections. The play contrasts those who have access to things that we, for the most part, take for granted: money, education, freedom, a voice in society, and those most basic of all needs, a place to sleep and food to put on the table... and those who can only dream of such things.

The Young Man at the end of the play expresses that, more than anything, what he wants to know are the 'secrets': that most fundamental of all secrets, how to live in the world, these secrets that he feels were never given to him, or that maybe he isn't 'allowed to know'. Here is a man that has never had the opportunity, the knowledge or the self-respect to make a life for himself—and the only way that he can make his way in the world is through a life of crime.

At the same time, our Rebel Leader has grown up without the basic rights we take for granted: the right to live in peace; the right to food and water and basic civil liberties; the right to live in a world without fear. The only option he feels he has left in order to hold his head up in the world, and to make his people's voice heard on the world stage, is to violently fight for these rights, even in a fight that is suicidal, and even in a fight that causes the same suffering to others that he has experienced all his life.

The scale is different, but it is the same universal suffering. The same cry for help. The same plea for understanding and compassion.

Personally, as a theatre director, I find the work fascinating not just because of its powerful and affecting story, but because of the bold and original form Bates uses to tell it. In the short, sharp sixty-minute rollercoaster ride of the play, there are only two scenes of what we would traditionally call 'dialogue' in the whole work. The work is almost choral in its construction, with four voices narrating both from within the action and from outside of it, and one of the play's great gifts is the musicality of the language throughout. The play has a rhythm, which is irrepressible, driving and compelling. The work requires the actors to narrate the story as themselves, as actors, often speaking in direct address to the audience, reporting action more often than enacting it. But they are also then required to transform into up to five or six different characters, changing often in a split-second, in front of their audience. This choice of form keeps the audience on the edge of the seat, as much as the action and tension of the story.

The other significant departure from traditional form in *Checklist for an Armed Robber* is that as the play simultaneously straddles two different worlds (Moscow and Newcastle), and jumps backwards and forwards in time and location, it is impossible to be overly-literal in the staging of the work. The two locations collide and blur repeatedly, we never remain in one location for long, and we, as an audience, are never allowed to get too comfortable.

As a result, the two 'dialogue' scenes in the work become in every way standout moments in the drama; both in terms of the form and action, these moments are the focal points of the unfolding drama. The first is the meeting and 'negotiation' between the Journalist and the Rebel Leader, the second is the confrontation and eventual negotiation between the Bookseller and the Young Man. The disparate outcomes of these negotiations is integral to the message of the play as a whole.

One of the most surprising aspects of this play for me is that there is so much humour and tenderness for what, on the surface, seems a very challenging theme. Another great surprise is that, despite its dark subject matter, the play provides a message of enduring hope and possibility in an otherwise potentially chilling theatrical experience. The play explores the interactions between aggressors and their victims, investigating two situations where the aggressor is confronted with the repercussions of their actions on their human targets. In the case of the Chechen rebels, a human face is put to their political ideals, and in the case of the Newcastle robber, this human connection leads to the crime being thwarted. It is a realisation that gives one cause for hope. If we can look behind the headlines, if we can see the person behind the action, as we do in reading or watching this play, then true understanding and connection is perhaps possible.

I have now had the good fortune to direct this play twice. After first tackling the work in Melbourne in mid-2007, I had the good fortune to bring the work to the stage for a second time in Fremantle in early 2009. It is a work that certainly warrants revisiting, and so I am very pleased that the theatre script is now being published so that the text can reach another even wider audience.

Chris Bendall
May 2009

Chris Bendall is currently Artistic Director of Deckchair Theatre, Fremantle and was Artistic Director of Theatre @ Risk, Melbourne until 2007.

PLAYWRIGHT'S NOTE

Checklist for an Armed Robber started life as two newspaper articles. In 2002, as part of the inaugural Blueprints Writers Assembly I was given a 'Responsive Project'. This entailed selecting a newspaper article from a given month, workshopping with a director and cast and then writing a script, culminating in a reading at the Sydney Theatre Company.

The month I'd been given was October and my 'responsive' week took place immediately after I had finished several difficult months writing for a TV show. My cunning plan was to write basic scenes and develop character notes *before* I walked into the workshop room. There was no way I was going to step foot in a room full of actors without the protection of reams of notes and, if I could manage it, a half-written script. As it was, I was so shattered after finishing work on the TV show I had no time at all to prepare. What I *did* have was an article about a journalist attempting to negotiate with the Chechen rebels who had taken over a Moscow theatre and another about a young man attempting to hold up a Newcastle bookshop. I could see some comparisons, in each case an older woman tried to negotiate with a younger armed man. One was successful, one was not. And both events happened over the same weekend. That was the start.

During that week we pulled apart these articles, the actors improvised around the action and created extraordinary characters. As a group we continued to research and every day people would bring in gruesome pictures from the web or related articles from magazines. We looked at the concept of courage, talked through moments of our own risk taking, of compassion, of personal danger and fear in our own lives and then began to work through the material we had. At the end of the week we had created a long improvisation that would become the spine of the Moscow story.

Several weeks of writing followed and the first draft of *Checklist for an Armed Robber* emerged, to be read at the STC Wharf 2. It was a tough audience, they had come to see UK writer Jimmy McGovern speak, but it was warmly received. And Jimmy liked it too.

As shocking as those events were in Moscow, I think in some naïve way I was doubly shocked they had happened in a theatre. It seemed unthinkable to me. A theatre was a safe space. A sacred space. That weekend showed me that there are no safe spaces. Fear, violence and cruelty exist everywhere. But so does courage. And compassion. And hope.

Since the play was first produced there has of course been more violence, more cruelty. More fear. The writer of one of the articles used in that long ago workshop, journalist Anna Politkovskaya, was shot dead in October 2006.

This play is dedicated to Anna and to others like her who champion courage, compassion and hope.

Vanessa Bates
July 2009

Checklist for an Armed Robber was first produced by Vitalstatistix Theatre at the Waterside Hall, Port Adelaide, 19 October 2005 with the following cast:

ACTOR 1, REBEL LEADER, ALEX, OWNER, REBEL, BOY, DERRICK, REPORTER 1	RomanVaculik
ACTOR 2, YOUNG MAN, NIKOLAI, REBEL, NIGEL, REPORTER 2	Nathan O'Keefe
ACTOR 3, JOURNALIST, RAISA, STAGE MANAGER, DRUNKEN WOMAN, REPORTER 3	Netta Yashchin
ACTOR 4, BOOK SELLER, LARISA, PRESENTER, REBEL, REPORTER 4, MOTHER	Astrid Pill

All other roles were performed by the company.

Director, Maude Davey
Designer, Cath Cantlon
Lighting Designer, Sue Grey-Gardner
Composer, Catherine Oates

CHARACTERS

The play is written for four actors, with doubling as follows:

Actor 1: REBEL LEADER, ALEX, BOOKSHOP OWNER, REBEL, BOY, DERRICK, REPORTER 1

Actor 2: YOUNG MAN, NIKOLAI, REBEL, NIGEL, REPORTER 2

Actor 3: JOURNALIST, RAISA, STAGE MANAGER, DRUNKEN WOMAN, REPORTER 3

Actor 4: BOOKSELLER, LARISA, PRESENTER, REBEL, REPORTER 4, MOTHER

PRODUCTION NOTE

There are a number of levels of reality and present time. Actors can become a character in the moment as well as a narrator or descriptor of the moment. At times this is also done in character.

At times, actors also play themselves, i.e. as actors discussing the situation, as in the opening lines.

At times there is an acknowledgement of an audience, for example the four hostages keep up a running commentary to an unseen listener throughout their ordeal, but at other times it is more conventional fourth wall stuff. Overlapping lines are used throughout the script. When a / occurs, the next line of dialogue overlaps.

Hostage characters (Raisa, Alex, Nikolai, Larisa) were not written with Russian accents in mind but rather the actors' own accent with the intention of making them almost part of the watching audience. (Having said that I have seen two productions where those characters were played with subtle Russian accents and it worked beautifully.)

The script is inspired by reported versions of two events that occurred within a couple of days of each other in Moscow and in Newcastle (Australia) in October 2002.

A small bell rings, the kind you hear tied to the door of a shop.

ACTOR 1: Saturday. October 26, 2002. Newcastle. Australia. Six-fifty p.m.

ACTOR 3: She would have been—well it's almost closing time, so she would have been thinking about... getting home, making dinner, whatever was on TV that night...

ACTOR 2: Bookshop. Mostly second-hand. A lot of New Age, heal-your-life stuff.

ACTOR 3: Anyway, it would have been sort of quiet. And if you've been doing that for so long it becomes second nature. / Packing up.

BOOKSELLER: [*listing*] Process and shelve any books that have come in that day, flag books that have been ordered, make sure they're on the shelf above the till...

ACTOR 1: Just a list of duties in your head that you tick off one by one.

BOOKSELLER: Go through the list of every book sold and ordered that day. Every book!

ACTOR 3: She's alone, don't forget. I mean she's used to it, yeah. But she's alone.

BOOKSELLER: Total and reconcile the eftpos machine. Turn the computer off. Set the answering machine. Set the alarm. Lock the door, closed sign, lights off!

People say to me: 'Ooh, must be lovely working in a bookshop. Get to read all day.'

She laughs to herself. A sound from somewhere in the shop. She looks up.

ACTOR 2: But let's go back a day.

ACTOR 1: Friday. October 25. Moscow. Russia. Two p.m.

ACTOR 4: The Palace of Culture! A gay nightclub, a cinema and the Dubrovka Theatre. Currently showing *Nord-Ost*, the first Russian musical based on the popular novel *The Two Captains*. They say it's a hit.

ACTOR 1: Fifty crew and front of house staff, thirty-five musicians, forty actors, seven hundred and fifty audience.

ACTOR 4: She enters the foyer. Lights out. Power cut—not sure if it was them or the police. She steps forward…

> The JOURNALIST *steps forward, she is in the foyer of the Dubrovka Theatre.*

JOURNALIST: And I feel, crunching underfoot, broken glass. A small noise. But in that enormous dark space, the sound reverberates. I look down. Amongst the glass… I begin to see small dropped items. A bag. A glove. A box of chocolates spilled amongst the spent cartridges. I walk slowly into the dark, calling as I go: 'Hello. Is anybody here? Anybody?'… And the light behind me fading and fading…

ACTOR 2: And we go back a day.

ACTOR 1: Thursday. October 24. Newcastle. Six-forty-five p.m.

ACTOR 3: He's got a gun. Sawn-off. Double-barrelled shotgun.

ACTOR 4: He likes this gun because it makes him feel bigger.

ACTOR 3: Bigger. And stronger. Like he knows what he's doing.

> *A* YOUNG MAN *steps forward.*

YOUNG MAN: I *do* know what I'm doing. [*Slight pause.*] Well you uncock it… it just cracks in half type of thing and there's a lever to do it. And you just put the shells in, crack it back up. There's two hammers on the back and you can pull them back and there's the double triggers too. / So you pull one of 'em, and one of 'em goes, and keep pulling—the other'll hammer as well.

ACTOR 1: He's got his gun, and he's got his place to hide and he's got some clothes to change into which he took off someone's clothes line.

YOUNG MAN: Or you do it straight at the same time, they both go down at once. Two shots.

ACTOR 3: He's already scouted the area and he's picked the place, he knows the routine and he's seen the lady who works there.

ACTOR 1: He knows he can do it.

YOUNG MAN: Bookshop.

BOOKSELLER: [*listing*] *Awaken the Giant Within, Empowerment Just*

Takes a Moment, How to Make Friends and Influence People, / *The Blue Day Book…*

ACTOR 3: Little place, edge of a shopping mall—there's a toilet there he can use.

ACTOR 1: And it's the last shop, almost, before the corner. He can duck down.

ACTOR 3: Snake his way home.

YOUNG MAN: Start the week before. Strap him in, under my jacket, make myself go for a little walk. Slowly make my way down the street till I'm there.

ACTOR 1: Heart races the whole way.

YOUNG MAN: Then run home. Then do it again.

ACTOR 3: Till he feels comfortable.

YOUNG MAN: Holding him. Walking with him under my clothes. Some I know—he's like their mate, their little dog.

ACTOR 3: The gun looks after them.

ACTOR 1: Speaks for them.

ACTOR 4: Does their dirty work.

YOUNG MAN: I go in the shop, suss the place. Feel what it's like to be standing there. Check it out—doors, till, window looking out on the street.

ACTOR 1: The owner sees him, becomes suspicious. [*As* BOOKSHOP OWNER] Are you right, mate?

YOUNG MAN: Yeah, thanks.

OWNER: Something I can help you with?

YOUNG MAN: No I'm just… looking.

OWNER: Looking for something special?

YOUNG MAN: No…

OWNER: You've been here a while. It's not a library, you know.

YOUNG MAN: I'm just looking!

OWNER: Well it's not a library. If you're not buying anything, you can go.

YOUNG MAN: Yeah. Alright.

He goes.

ACTOR 3: Think about it a bit.

YOUNG MAN: Yeah.

ACTOR 4: Think about doing another B and E instead. Easy.

YOUNG MAN: Yeah, I know.

ACTOR 3: Jewellery maybe. Wallet. Phone someone's left lying on the kitchen table.

YOUNG MAN: Think about giving it up or finding another place or waiting a bit so he forgets my face. But the thing is I can't wait. Saturday. Want to do it. Have to.

ACTOR 1: Walk home. Gun's heavy.

ACTOR 4: Need practice. Psych up.

ACTOR 1: This will be his first armed robbery.

YOUNG MAN: Walk home. Look out for things that can help me… [*Pointing them out*] Rubbish tins to chuck me clothes… back lane there to duck through… mate's fence to jump over if I have to. It's all planned out. I know what I'm doing.

ACTOR 1: This will be his *first* armed robbery.

ACTOR 3: But we go back a day.

Pause.

ACTOR 4: Wednesday. October 23. Moscow. Ten p.m.

ACTOR 2: *Nord-Ost*. They say it's a hit. Tonight for instance. Seven hundred and fifty in the audience.

ACTOR 1: And more not yet counted. He is among them. Still. In the shadows. Quiet as a mouse.

ACTOR 2: *Nôtre Dame de Paris* and *Les Mis* have also been playing in Moscow.

REBEL LEADER: But *Nord-Ost* is a home-grown hit. A Russian hit. And that's why we are here.

STAGE MANAGER: [*Possibly British accent, calm, precise*] As stage manager I do the calls for the actors. I let them know how long they've got, from the half-hour call all the way to beginners… which is five minutes till curtain. It's up to me to make sure they're on time and in place.

Natalia Novikova as Stage Manager in the 2007 Theatre@Risk production.
(Photo: Josephine Harkin)

REBEL LEADER: Go over the list in my head. Make sure we're on time and in place.

STAGE MANAGER: I also do the calls for the orchestra. They get a first and second call.

REBEL LEADER: Explosives. Weapons. Personnel. Behind doors and above walls.

STAGE MANAGER: We also have the maestro's call and etiquette says he has to be fetched. [*Correcting herself*] Or she.

REBEL LEADER: There is an adjoining passage with the nightclub and many of us are here. In black and khaki, hands full, faces hidden. Waiting.

STAGE MANAGER: *Nord-Ost* has thirty-five musicians and I do *not* let them start tuning until every single one of them is in my sights. Their cue is fifty percent house lights. Tuning… is an automatic response. Once you've set them off you can't stop them.

REBEL LEADER: So. Here we are.

ACTOR 2: Listening as the audience mingles in the foyer.

ACTOR 4: As the actors do their final preparations backstage.

STAGE MANAGER: [*announcing*] Ladies and gentlemen of the cast, *Nord-Ost*, this is your five-minute call. Five-minute call.

REBEL LEADER: Explosives. Weapons. Personnel. Waiting.

ACTOR 4: Listening. As the audience purchase their chocolates, / their programs, their drinks.

ACTOR 2: Listening. To the actors, their warm-up, their make-up, their lace-up of boots and bonnet and bodice…

REBEL LEADER: In black and khaki, hands full, faces hidden. Waiting.

ACTOR 2: In the bathroom. They wash their hands, discuss the show, fix their lipstick, check their teeth. Make their mobile phone calls.

ACTOR 4: In the dressing-room. They whisper, they gargle, they inhale and ingest, props check, radio mike check. Make their mobile phone calls.

ACTOR 2: The young man stands in front of his mirror. Psyching up. Pretending. Playing a part. [*As* YOUNG MAN, *making a pretend phone call*] Yeah hi, is Kelly there? Right… Hi Kelly. Just wanted

Tim Solly as the Young Man in the 2009 Deckchair Theatre production.
(Photo: Jon Green)

to tell you you're a fucking bitch. I fucking hate you. And you're gonna fucking get it.

ACTOR 3: He's too nervous to make the real call.

YOUNG MAN: [*in despair*] Gutless.

REBEL LEADER: On time and in place.

ACTOR 4: Ready.

ACTOR 3: Ready.

ACTOR 2: Ready.

STAGE MANAGER: [*announcing*] Ladies and gentlemen of the orchestra, this is your second and final call. Second and final call.

REBEL LEADER: I dream of dying on a battlefield. [*Pause.*] Ready.

STAGE MANAGER: [*announcing*] Ladies and gentlemen of the cast, *Nord-Ost*, Act Two beginners please.

ACTOR 1: Interval bell rings.

ACTOR 2: Lights change.

ACTOR 3: Tuning sounds.

ACTOR 4: Audience begin to return to their seats…

> *The four audience members find their places.* RAISA, *middle-aged, well-dressed, is on her mobile phone.*

RAISA: … because it's his choice, that's why. Don't. Look… it's starting. We'll talk when I get home. Don't you—

> *But he has hung up.*

I was supposed to come tonight with my husband… and we had an argument. And he stayed at home.

> LARISA *is a young woman, excited to be here, looking forward to meeting the stars.*

LARISA: My friend's in the chorus. I've seen it already, opening night. But, um, she's a swing for one of the small roles—she gets a solo tonight, so I'm here. We're going out after the show, she's got a friend who plays a soldier. I dunno how that'll work out. I'm here for her really. But, ah… he's quite nice…

> NIKOLAI, *a middle-aged man, flips through the program patiently. He's enduring the show for the sake of his wife.*

NIKOLAI: Just reading the lyrics in the program. The company I work for was given tickets for tonight. Wife had a headache—stayed home. Very disappointed. I'll take the program for her. Shame. She's the musical theatre buff, not me.

ALEX, mid twenties, bored and restless.

ALEX: I know this girl in the box office. She gave me a freebie. Um… First half was pretty dull. About fifty people left at interval. I thought… nah, it's cold outside. My honest opinion? I reckon the book's better.

The YOUNG MAN *makes the real phone call. Nervous. Polite.*

YOUNG MAN: Yeah… can I speak to Kelly please? Please? Oh right. Yeah okay. Could you tell her I called? I just want to know how she's going. Can you tell her… I miss her? Thanks.

In the theatre, soldiers have begun to enter. The audience look around, confused. Overlap:

ALEX: Soldiers! /

RAISA: Soldiers running up the aisles. / Waving guns. Is it real?

LARISA: Soldiers running through the auditorium.

NIKOLAI: Part of the show? / They did this in *Cats*.

The REBEL LEADER *steps forward. He is young, late twenties, this responsibility sits heavily with him.*

REBEL LEADER: Ladies and gentlemen, stay seated / please.

NIKOLAI: Watching him. Like another actor. Note he's holding an AK47 / assault rifle.

REBEL LEADER: Nobody get up. Nobody leave.

NIKOLAI: Magazine capacity: thirty rounds.

REBEL LEADER: This audience is now surrounded.

NIKOLAI: Sighting range: eight hundred metres.

REBEL LEADER: We are armed.

NIKOLAI: Killing range: fifteen hundred metres.

REBEL LEADER: We *will* shoot.

LARISA: [*panicking*] This isn't part of the show. I've seen the show, this isn't part of it.

RAISA: Don't... draw attention to yourself.

LARISA: I want to stand up! I want to walk out of here. They've got no *right*.

RAISA: Shh! They'll see you.

REBEL LEADER: Ladies and gentlemen. There are fifty of us here today. We are from Chechnya. / There is a war there.

LARISA: I think about getting up, getting up and running in that first moment, but it's useless.

REBEL LEADER: We have now brought that war here to Moscow.

RAISA: They're armed to the teeth with guns, / grenades, homemade bombs packed with nails and bits of metal.

REBEL LEADER: We are demanding of President Putin: Curtailment of the war and beginning of the immediate withdrawal of Russian aggressors from Chechnya.

NIKOLAI: They've wired explosives to the walls and to the doors / in case the military try something.

STAGE MANAGER: Every single one of them must be in your sights.

REBEL LEADER: You are our hostages. Remain calm. Remain seated.

STAGE MANAGER: Once you've set them off you can't stop them.

REBEL LEADER: We are not monsters. We are not terrorists. [*With a laugh*] If we were we'd ask for a plane and a million dollars!

Hostages stretch. Try to get comfortable. Time passes.

NIKOLAI: A couple of the women have radios and we can hear news reports—that's how we know what's going on. [*Nodding, with contempt*] Yes. Some of them are women.

RAISA: They sit so quietly. Along the edge of the auditorium.

LARISA: Like they're part of the audience.

RAISA: The men roam freely, laugh, make jokes. But the women. They wait. And they listen.

Everyone listens for news. Radio static. Ridiculous BBC World Service type accents.

DERRICK: [*radio*] And it's back to our journalist who is standing outside the Dubrovka Theatre. How is it, Nigel? What's the current situation?

NIGEL: [*radio*] Yes, Derrick, I spoke to a man earlier who didn't know about the situation. He in turn spoke to a woman who also didn't know. The situation at this moment is unclear and the chances of it getting clearer in the future look very murky indeed.

DERRICK: [*radio*] Now crossing live to some people who have been watching closely for several hours and claim to have no idea what's going on. But what we do know is: At ten-fifteen on Wednesday night...

The following, fast, stupid, a range of news broadcast accents:

REPORTER 1: [*radio*] Fifty Chechen gunmen!

REPORTER 2: [*radio*] Fifty-five hostage takers!

REPORTER 3: [*radio*] Forty-one hostage takers—nineteen of whom were *women*...

REPORTER 4: [*radio*] ... eighteen of whom were female suicide bombers...

REPORTER 2: [*radio*] ... purdah-clad women...

REPORTER 3: [*radio*] ... female accomplices strapped with explosives...

REPORTER 2: [*radio*] ... stormed the theatre...

REPORTER 3: [*radio*] ... burst on the stage...

REPORTER 4: [*radio*] ... swept down the aisles...

REPORTER 2: [*radio*] ... lined the walls...

REPORTER 3: [*radio*] ... swung from the ceiling...

The voices have changed, earnest BBC or CNN clones into mocking REBELS.

REBEL 1: [*with a snicker*] ... terror merchants...

REBEL 2: ... men in camouflage...

REBEL 3: ... a hundred suicidal Chechen terrorists...

Laughter.

REBEL 1: ... a vicious band of callous gunmen...

More laughter. It dies off. RAISA *looks around her grimly.*

RAISA: The Chechens are in fits of laughter at the descriptions of themselves.

ALEX: They're not so bad. The one without a mask... he jokes... he makes us laugh...

LARISA: And then he shoots a woman.

To the surprise of the audience and the rebels, a WOMAN *enters the auditorium.*

WOMAN: Hey! When's the fucking show start?

NIKOLAI: [*shocked*] A woman has just... walked in through the door of the theatre! How the hell did she... aren't they guarding the doors?

LARISA: [*turning to look*] My God. She's *drunk*...

The REBEL LEADER *stands up.*

REBEL LEADER: Hey! No-one said you could get up.

WOMAN: Fuck you... I bought my ticket. [*Pointing at an empty seat*] There's my seat.

REBEL LEADER: [*realising*] You were not here before. Who are you? How did you get in?

The WOMAN *hesitates slightly.*

WOMAN: Through the fucking door! Geez! You people sell the champagne... you expect us to guzzle it all in ten minutes? Glug glug glug...

LARISA: The Chechens whisper together. They're confused... they don't know how she got in.

WOMAN: Glug glug glug...

NIKOLAI: They think she could be secret police. FSB.

WOMAN: FSB! In these shoes? You're joking.

She looks around at them.

LARISA: Don't make them angry, please.

WOMAN: Fuck this, I'm going.

REBEL LEADER: Stay where you are.

WOMAN: Why? What are you going to do? Shoot me?

She turns away.

LARISA: And he did. In the back. She fell and they took her away. Was she dead? Wounded? No-one knew.

RAISA: Until they took us to the washrooms. Her body, slung in a corner. Blood smeared across the tiles where they had dragged her. No more jokes.

> The REBEL LEADER *stands on the stage. The audience watch him, fearful.*

REBEL LEADER: [*sternly*] Take out all papers and passports. We will now sort you into nationality. Foreigners will be released. Children will be released. If you have mobile phones you may use them. I suggest that you ask your loved ones to organise protests on your behalf. Protest the occupation of Chechnya by Russian forces. And the government-sanctioned criminal behaviour of the occupying troops.

> *A beat and then they all take out their mobile phones and make frantic calls.*

> The YOUNG MAN *finally manages to speak to his girlfriend.*

YOUNG MAN: Kelly? Yeah it's me. How are you? And the baby? Yeah… I just… someone told me where you were staying. No… I… I just wanted you to know… I'm getting some money together. Oh… job. Yeah. Bookshop. Don't laugh. [*Laughing*] It's not bullshit. [*He stops laughing.*] Who the fuck told you that? Kelly?

[*As* ACTOR] But she's hung up. He calls again, trying to keep a lid on his temper.

JOURNALIST: [*as* ACTOR] The journalist's phone rings. Los Angeles. One a.m. [*As* JOURNALIST, *sleepily*] Hello? Yes this is she. Who is this? [*She sits up, awake.*] I'm not *in* Moscow.

YOUNG MAN: God this fucking town *talks*. It's a shotgun. I only want it for a little while. While I get myself sorted.

JOURNALIST: What do they want me to do? [*Slight pause.*] Negotiate? I'm a journalist. A *Russian* journalist. [*Pause.*] Yes, I have some… understanding for their cause. So do others.

YOUNG MAN: I'm doing this for you.

JOURNALIST: I can get a flight in a few hours.

YOUNG MAN: You and Luke.

JOURNALIST: I'll be in Moscow Thursday morning. Wait… my family…

But they have hung up. She stares at the phone.

YOUNG MAN: Kelly... Can I come and see you? Please?

JOURNALIST: The first time...

YOUNG MAN: *Please?* Please, Kelly.

JOURNALIST: The first time my son checked under our car for a bomb he was seven years old.

YOUNG MAN: He's my son too.

He hangs up. Frustrated.

ACTOR 4: Thursday. October 24. Moscow. Six a.m.

RAISA *puts up her hand. Talks to (unseen) rebel.*

RAISA: Excuse me. I have to go to the toilet. Can I go to the toilet? [*Slight pause.*] What?

LARISA: [*whispering, aware of the watching rebels*] What is it?

RAISA: He's saying—no-one is to leave the theatre. We have to stay here.

ALEX: [*to the rebel, helpfully*] They took us before to the washrooms. In groups.

RAISA: I have to go. I have to... [*Shocked*] They say we have to use the orchestra pit.

LARISA: What?

RAISA: The orchestra pit. They say no-one is to leave the theatre.

ALEX: [*to the rebel*] Surely there's some other place? No?

RAISA: I can't... I can't do that. [*Suddenly, to* LARISA] Come with me.

LARISA: [*very unwilling*] No! They won't let us.

ALEX: [*to the rebel*] Can they go together?

RAISA: [*to* ALEX] Will they let us go together? [*To* LARISA] Please come... I'm so scared...

LARISA: He'll say no...

ALEX: He said yes. You can go together.

RAISA *clutches at* LARISA *who is unable to resist. Under the eye of the rebels they make their way to the orchestra pit.*

Caitlin Bereseford-Ord as Bookseller and Brendan Hanson as Alex in the
2009 Deckchair Theatre production. (Photo: Nick Merrylees)

LARISA: *I'm sorry, excuse me, thank you.* Squeezing past the legs of other hostages. All the time, feeling them watch me. From the stage, the balcony, the aisles. Watch us. *I'm sorry, excuse me, thank you…*

RAISA: I don't know whether to crumble or to stand up and shout… I don't care! Whether I should just squat down and… defecate on the floor, be proud that I can do it… or whether I should feel ashamed that these people can see me. I am so glad this lady came with me, I feel… if we're together it will be alright.

She tries to squat on the floor. LARISA *looks the other way.*

LARISA: This is *sooo* embarrassing.

RAISA: [*to* LARISA] We don't have anything, we don't have any tissues. Do you have some tissues?

LARISA: No.

RAISA: Why can't they take us to the toilet? What's wrong with the toilet? We went to the toilet before, I don't understand why we can't go to the toilet. I don't have tissues. I don't have any tissues. I can't go back like this…

LARISA: Here.

She holds something out to RAISA.

My program.

RAISA *slowly takes it from her.*

RAISA: It's been signed.

LARISA: [*with a shrug*] I have a friend in the cast. Look… that's her there.

RAISA: Oh. I…

A delicate pause.

LARISA: It's okay. She hates that photo.

They laugh faintly, fearfully, as RAISA *tears at the paper. Only slight relief. They are terrified and near tears.*

ALEX: The women now wear headphones to listen to their radios— we're not allowed to listen anymore.

NIKOLAI: And… they're knitting. Knitting. They have to negotiate their knitting over the explosives sitting in their laps. I hope they don't get their wool mixed up with their wires.

Caitlin Beresford-Ord (left) as Larisa and Vivienne Garrett as Raisa in the 2009 Deckchair Theatre production. (Photo: Jon Green)

You know? Knit one, purl one, [*shouting suddenly*] boom!

Los Angeles. An American PRESENTER *taps a mike and clears her throat to engage attention. Overlap...*

PRESENTER: Ladies and gentlemen. Welcome to Los Angeles. Tonight's guest was scheduled to receive an award for courage in journalism.

YOUNG MAN: You've got different types of shells. Twelve-gauge. Eighteen-gauge. Up to thirty-six-gauge. Higher the gauge the more gunpowder / and the more... little lead pellets.

PRESENTER: Instead she flew home early this morning to help in negotiations with Chechen rebels who are holding up to seven hundred people hostage / in a Moscow theatre.

YOUNG MAN: They're not accurate. They're designed to spray. You'll just as likely miss from say a hundred metres away. But up close I've seen 'em do some awful damage. Exit wound's worse than the entry wound. [*Pause.*] Tears everything on the way out.

PRESENTER: Our thoughts and prayers are with her.

The YOUNG MAN *looks at himself in his mirror.*

YOUNG MAN: Fucking useless. Piece of shit. What do you know?

He slams at the wall beside the mirror.

The jingle of the shop bell. Newcastle.

BOOKSELLER: [*cheerful*] I like working on a Saturday. No, I *do*.

YOUNG MAN: [*quiet*] She's in there.

BOOKSELLER: Alright, if it's a beautiful day outside, that's... yes alright, that's a bit hard to take.

YOUNG MAN: Stand on the street outside like I'm waiting for a bus. Watch her. Through the glass.

BOOKSELLER: [*laughing*] No-one likes being shut away in a dark room, do they? But it's not like I'm a prisoner.

YOUNG MAN: All alone.

BOOKSELLER: [*laughing*] A lot of people like to browse on a Saturday. Saturday's good for browsing.

And you get a lot of interesting people in a bookshop.

YOUNG MAN: I know what I'm doing.

BOOKSELLER: Everyone's looking for something special.

The hostages curl in their seats, try to get comfortable. Fail.

ALEX: They said they'll let the children go, but there are still children here. They said they'll let the foreigners go, but there are still foreigners here. They said they'll release us soon, but now they say they came here to die. So / we wait.

RAISA: We wait. Sitting, hunched in our seats.

NIKOLAI: Thirsty. Hungry.

RAISA: Too scared to sleep.

ALEX: The smell is… Those closest to the orchestra pit are sweating with the stench of it.

JOURNALIST: I rang my husband. My children. To tell them where I was going. What I was trying to do. [*Pause.*] They understand. [*Pause.*] I'm not sure I do.

BOOKSELLER: [*laughing*] No-one likes being shut away in a dark room, do they? But it's not like I'm a prisoner.

YOUNG MAN: Exit wound's worse than the entry wound. Tears everything on the way out.

ACTOR 3: Friday. October 25. Moscow. Midday.

LARISA: [*almost in another world*] If I close my eyes… and rest my head in my arms, so my ears are covered… and I block my nose… I can almost pretend I'm not in a theatre. I'm not in a siege. I'm not surrounded by gunmen. I'm not five seats away from a woman with explosives strapped to her waist. [*Pause.*] I'm not here at all.

REBEL LEADER: [*smiling, a treat*] Ladies and gentlemen.

The audience members stir and watch, apprehensive.

NIKOLAI: Look at him. He's positively preening. The combat pants. The assault rifle. He loves it up there. Centre stage.

REBEL LEADER: In a few minutes a camera crew will be coming into the theatre. Television. Stay in your seats. No talking. [*A little joke*] Just sit and look beautiful.

LARISA: [*bleakly*] I want them to film me.

NIKOLAI: Shhh.

LARISA: I want my dad to see me…

RAISA: [*hissing*] They said not to speak.

> *The audience members watch eagerly as a camera crew circles them.*

ALEX: Cameraman circling the audience. Filming us. Row after row of blank scared faces.

NIKOLAI: Showing the position of the bombs, the guards, the wiring around the walls. Maybe the Chechens think… he's just filming us, but I can see what he's doing.

RAISA: I can't help feeling… ashamed. The smell of us.

LARISA: I want them to film me. I want my dad to see me. I want him to come and get me.

NIKOLAI: In the right hands this footage is very useful for our… rescue.

RAISA: If they asked for this, if this is one of their demands, then this is good because it means the government are giving them what they want. Letting them tell the world. And if that's what they want… / this is good.

ALEX: They're asking to speak to a hostage. The crew are asking for one of us to speak.

NIKOLAI: The one without the mask agrees.

ALEX: [*looking around*] No-one's volunteering. No-one's talking.

RAISA: I don't want to stand. I don't want to do anything that will draw attention to me. I don't want to be a spokesperson if… if everyone else is sitting, I'm not… I'm not stupid.

> *Suddenly,* LARISA *stands up.*

LARISA: Me!

> *The other hostages respond to her.*

> RAISA *tries to persuade her to sit down.* NIKOLAI *suggests he will go instead.* ALEX *reaches to touch her, reassure her… she shakes them all off.*

[*Calmly*] My name is Larisa. I am a student. My languages are Russian. English. French… some German. I will speak with you.

Pause, then...

ALEX: She stumbles from her seat. Two rebels escort her away.

RAISA: I watch her yellow blouse as she follows him up the aisle. She seems tiny. And then... she's gone.

The BOOKSELLER *steps forward.*

BOOKSELLER: Newcastle's a lovely city. We do have a lot of history. Coal, steel... Of course some wonderful actors have come out of this area. [*Thinking*] John Bell... Yahoo Serious...

YOUNG MAN: [*on the phone*] Yeah... can I speak to Kelly please? Please? / Oh right.

BOOKSELLER: Lot of ex-Novocastrians like to come back. Settle down. Have a family. / It's that sort of place.

YOUNG MAN: Could you tell her I called? / I just want to know how she's going.

Can you tell her... I miss her? And Luke. Thanks.

He hangs up.

BOOKSELLER: So you've got the harbour, and the lighthouse, and the breakwater. Beautiful beaches. King Edward Park. And the brewery, and the Queen's Wharf as opened by the Queen. What else do you want to see?

YOUNG MAN: All I see is me, in this moment. Getting ready. Getting set. I try and see myself with the gun, imagine her face, her fear. She hands over the till nice and easy and I'm gone. But I can't. All I see is me. And this moment.

ACTOR 1: Friday. October 25. Moscow. Two p.m.

The JOURNALIST *in the theatre foyer, as in the opening scene.*

JOURNALIST: I walk slowly into the dark, calling as I go: 'Hello. Is anybody here? Anybody?...' And the light behind me fading and fading. I pass the theatre cloakroom, full of coats, umbrellas...

ACTOR 2: Furs, wraps, cloaks, hats.

JOURNALIST: Like walking through a museum at night. I see evidence that people once lived all around me. Relics, discarded... the cold, fossilised remnants of a civilisation that has ceased to exist. And the silence...

She begins to look around, she is in the theatre foyer outside the auditorium.

[*Calling*] Hello? You asked me to come. To talk with your commander… [*To the audience*] As I call out, I move slowly up the stairs. Step into a space, dimly lit.

ACTOR 2: A foyer, a waiting room, a place to come at interval, discuss the first act, / glass of bubbly…

ACTOR 1: Yes, the chorus are terrific but the lead male sucks…

ACTOR 4: … buy chocolates, read a program, ring your babysitter…

JOURNALIST: Empty. Silent. Try to listen for some clue. Aware that beyond the theatre doors, seven hundred hostages are listening too.

A REBEL *appears in the foyer, pushing* LARISA *before him. She is subdued.*

A man appears…

REBEL: Black mask. Khaki shirt. Machine gun.

JOURNALIST: Gripping the arm of a young woman.

LARISA: Yellow blouse. White face. Want my father.

JOURNALIST: Straighten up, project calm. [*To* REBEL] I am here to meet with your commander.

The REBEL *nods, acknowledges. The* JOURNALIST *reaches for* LARISA. *Briefly touches her.*

[*To* LARISA] Are you alright?

Slight pause.

LARISA: I want my father.

The REBEL *pushes her away. The* JOURNALIST *turns back, feeling helpless.*

JOURNALIST: What can I do?

YOUNG MAN: [*to his mirror*] Worthless. / Piece of shit.

JOURNALIST: Helpless…

YOUNG MAN: Hopeless. / Just do it.

JOURNALIST: My God.

REBEL 2: Oy! You!

The JOURNALIST *looks around.*

JOURNALIST: [*to the audience*] More men. Masked, peering down from the balconies above.

REBEL 3: You! Writer! Will you write about us?

JOURNALIST: Yes. [*To the audience*] They seem pleased at the thought.

REBEL 2: Will it be published back home?

JOURNALIST: I don't know. Perhaps. [*To the audience*] I can see through their mouth slits—they're actually… smiling at me.

REBEL 3: Will you put it on the internet?

JOURNALIST: [*to the audience*] They sound so… pleased with themselves. A little scared. But above all. Young. [*To the* REBELS] It's not up to me, but yes, if I can, I will. Let me ask you something… your mothers. Do your mothers know about this?

REBEL 2: None of our families know. Or at least they didn't. They probably know now.

REBEL 3: It makes no difference. We can't go back now. Either the war stops, or…

Slight pause. REBEL 3 *makes an explosion gesture with his hands.*

[*Quietly*] Boom.

JOURNALIST: [*to the audience*] Silence. [*To the* REBELS] When will the commander come?

The REBELS *shift. The good humour has gone.*

REBEL 2: In a hurry, is she?

REBEL 3: Doesn't like the theatre? Culture snob!

REBEL 2: Everything happens in good time. Sit. Wait. Like the rest of us.

She does.

In the bookshop, the BOOKSELLER *is ticking off books against her order list. The* YOUNG MAN *tries to psych himself up.*

YOUNG MAN: No job. No girl. No baby. You got nothing. You're worth nothing. / Piece of shit. Stupid. Useless. Worthless.

BOOKSELLER: *Awaken the Giant Within*; *Empowerment Just Takes a Moment*; *How to Make Friends and Influence People… The Blue Day Book.*

Brendan Hanson as the Rebel Leader in the 2009 Deckchair Theatre production. (Photo: Jon Green)

ACTOR 2: Checks one last time, the gun slid down his shirt, the Coles plastic bag stuffed in one pocket. His heart pounds, his skin sweats. [*As* YOUNG MAN] Now *do* it. Get in there. [*As* ACTOR 2] This will be his *first* armed robbery.

> *Jingle of the shop bell. The* YOUNG MAN, *nervous, appears in the shop. Casually browsing, he keeps an eye on the* BOOKSELLER *as he does so.*

BOOKSELLER: *The Seven Habits of Highly Effective People*; *I'm OK, You're OK*… [*She hears a noise. Friendly*] Is someone there?

> *The two scenes overlap. In Moscow, the* REBEL LEADER *approaches the* JOURNALIST, *holding out a hand. He is calm, courteous, at times charming.*

REBEL LEADER: Deputy commander of the subversion and intelligence battalion. Apologies for the delay.

JOURNALIST: Journalist. Apology accepted.

BOOKSELLER: Can I help you?

JOURNALIST: Why are you doing this?

YOUNG MAN: Oh… I'm just looking, thanks.

REBEL LEADER: You of all people know what has driven us here.

BOOKSELLER: Take your time, love. These booklists go on and on.

JOURNALIST: You seem so young. You, and the ones who have spoken to me. Such young voices.

REBEL LEADER: [*with a wry laugh*] Twenty-nine is old in Chechen years. If I am alive in ten years time, I'll be ancient. My generation have lived through two wars. We grow up knowing nothing but fighting. All we want is for that fighting to stop.

BOOKSELLER: *Rich Dad, Poor Dad*; *The Power of Positive Thinking*; *The Art of Happiness*…

JOURNALIST: Difficult perhaps for some people to imagine…

REBEL LEADER: The suffering of others?

JOURNALIST: Do you dream of peace?

REBEL LEADER: [*with a wry smile*] For the first time in many years, I feel… peace.

In the hour when we took the theatre, I walked around the stage, and behind. The dressing-rooms. Workshops and wardrobe rooms. All silent.

Strange to see—painted scenes, bright costumes and wooden swords, empty suitcases. All waiting for the show to continue.

A silent space… seems empty… but full of story.

JOURNALIST: And now you are… actors in the story.

REBEL LEADER: Yes. And thanks to you… our audience is the whole world. They watch us—with our wooden swords and empty suitcases—and the story will continue. And these actors will fall down and die, but there will be more actors. Always, more actors.

JOURNALIST: But… in this story, it's not just you acting a part.

REBEL LEADER: No… it's regrettable…

JOURNALIST: Out there, hundreds of people, frightened, hungry…

REBEL LEADER: Yes.

JOURNALIST: Let the children go. What part must they play in all of this?

REBEL LEADER: We have let the young children go…

JOURNALIST: I saw a girl, just now. A young girl. A teenager. Barely more than a child herself.

REBEL LEADER: Our children, our teenagers who are barely more than children, have been suffering for years / at the hands of your people.

JOURNALIST: Their parents, sick with worry and fear, / stand on the street outside.

REBEL LEADER: As our parents are sick with worry and fear.

JOURNALIST: I saw a woman crying loudly, hysterically; she let her daughter attend tonight's show / as a present for her sixteenth birthday.

REBEL LEADER: I see women cry like that too, as their sons and their husbands are dragged away to be tortured, their daughters raped, their belongings burnt. Some of those women are here today. Guarding hostages.

JOURNALIST: It's revenge then? Our children, their children. Our pain, their pain. It never stops.

REBEL LEADER: It stops when our demands are met or when we detonate the bombs. That's when it stops for us. But the rest? That's up to Russia.

Putin can remove his military from Chechnya. That is his choice. This, is *our* choice.

You speak well. But I know we are surrounded by more than just crying parents. We will never walk free from this building.

JOURNALIST: It could be tomorrow. Are you prepared for that?

REBEL LEADER: Yes. You asked about my dreams—I dream of dying on a battlefield. Not amongst civilians.

JOURNALIST: Why am I here? To negotiate, you said. What is there to negotiate? I am a writer. I write about suffering, that's why I write about your homeland. I try and speak for those without a voice. But right now, through that door, seven hundred people sit in silence and I can do nothing for them. Nothing.

Pause. The REBEL LEADER *regards her. She wonders if she has gone too far.*

ACTOR 2: The young man walks around the bookshop. Feels for his gun.

BOOKSELLER: You right there, love?

YOUNG MAN: Um… yeah… just looking.

BOOKSELLER: Well you look as long as you like, love. Don't rush. That's half the pleasure.

The YOUNG MAN *pulls back, confused. Moves around the books again. Picks one up.*

REBEL LEADER: Alright. Come back. In one hour. You can bring… water. Enough for everyone here.

JOURNALIST: You're taking a risk.

REBEL LEADER: Only you. Only what you can carry.

JOURNALIST: I understand. They will be grateful.

REBEL LEADER: One hour.

JOURNALIST: Thank you. [*To us*] And that's it. Meeting over. Permission to bring water.

She leaves him. The REBEL LEADER *addresses his followers.*

REBEL LEADER: Get them food. Whatever you can find.

A shower of candy is thrown at the hostages. They dive for it.

RAISA: It was peanut brittle. [*Fast*] I nearly didn't eat it… I nearly didn't… It could be poison or something. But then I looked and it's from the candy bar. I thought it looked good before but I didn't buy it then because—I thought it was too expensive. The mark-up they put on food at the theatre. It's criminal… And now a piece has been thrown at me… /

It was the best peanut brittle I have ever eaten.

ALEX: Peanut brittle! Ha! Think about it! Think what it means! [*Triumphantly*] If they're feeding us, they can't be going to kill us! Can they?

    Slight pause.

This is going to make me thirsty, isn't it? That's why / they've done it…

NIKOLAI: Two squares of chocolate. Think… of the hands that threw them to me.

LARISA: Trying to suck on it really slowly.

NIKOLAI: Think… that the burst of energy it will give me is completely useless.

LARISA: [*tearfully*] Trying to taste something… sweet on my tongue.

ALEX: [*calmly*] I'm so fucking scared. And I'm so fucking *tired* of being scared. My whole body aches with being too scared to move.

    Pause. Overlapping:

YOUNG MAN: Checklist for an armed robber: Plastic bag. Change of clothes. Double-barrelled shotgun. The night before: Keep busy, talk to your mates about anything else. Ring your ex-girlfriend. Plead with her. / Abuse her. Tell her you love her. That morning; Check that the mate will be in.

JOURNALIST: Checklist for a sympathetic journalist: Notebook. Ticket from LA to Moscow. Bottled water. The night before: Ring your husband. / Ring your children. Ring your editor. Check your will.

REBEL LEADER: Checklist for a rebel leader: Three minivans. One hundred and fourteen hand grenades. Fifteen assault rifles. / Eleven pistols. Twenty-five belt pouches with explosives. Two forty-kilo self-made bombs. Thirty mines and booby traps. The night before: Wait. Listen. Pray.

BOOKSELLER: Checklist for a bookshop manager: Total and reconcile till. Total and reconcile eftpos machine. Process and shelve any books that have come in that day, flag books that have been ordered. The night before: A light dinner, a little telly, an uninterrupted sleep.

Pause.

ACTOR 2: Saturday. October 26. Moscow. Three a.m. The hostages try to sleep. But a young man, just a boy really, is arguing with his mother.

BOY: Can't sleep.

MOTHER: Shhhh. Try, my darling.

BOY: I'm thirsty… my water bottle is empty…

MOTHER: I know, my love, please, please, quiet now…

BOY: It *stinks*. This whole place stinks.

MOTHER: [*panicked*] Dear God… Please, darling don't, you'll wake them, you'll wake them up, shhh… [*As* ACTOR] And she tries to keep him calm and quiet, she tries desperately because this is the third day of the siege and there is no more water, or peanut brittle or chocolate squares, there are no more jokes or friendly chats with the rebels, only fear like a coiled wire twisting tighter and tighter till just one small thing sets it off…

The BOY *stands up and shouts:*

BOY: I never wanted to come to this *stupid* show in the first place!

REBEL: A rebel stands up and stares at the boy. Raises his gun in warning.

MOTHER: Please no! No… I beg you…

[*As* ACTOR] But she can't stop it and she watches as her son throws his water bottle through the air, hitting the head of one of them…

BOY: I hope it hurts! I hope he bleeds!…

REBEL: … and then the shots begin.

ACTOR 3: Bang!

ACTOR 4: Bang!

ACTOR 2: Bang!

> *The* REBEL LEADER *looks up, alarmed.*

REBEL LEADER: Stop! What are you doing? You fool. It's just a kid! [*As* ACTOR] But he feels the panic well up around him...

RAISA: [*pointing, in shock*] Her son! My God! They shot him!...

LARISA: I'm glad my mouth was so dry because I might have shouted in shock. They're talking with each other, getting angry. Maybe they want to shoot us all now. Or maybe they didn't want to shoot anyone and now they have, so...

RAISA: I can't believe those women let that happen. Are none of them mothers? None of them went to him. None of them picked him up. [*She cries.*] My God!

> *She stands up, goes towards the child. The* REBEL LEADER *turns on her. She cowers.*

REBEL LEADER: Sit down!

RAISA: The boy's hurt. He's bleeding.

REBEL LEADER: Sit down or I will shoot!

> RAISA *drops fearfully back into her seat.*

[*As* ACTOR] And as the sound of the shots still echo around the room, he wonders if this is the beginning of the end. [*As* REBEL LEADER *to the hostages*] Everyone! Stay calm. Remain seated!

NIKOLAI: I thought I realised the danger and I realised the seriousness, but it was like it was happening around me... like a show.

REBEL LEADER: Do not get up! / Remain seated!

NIKOLAI: I see these people are killers, they don't give a shit about us, we are nothing to them, nothing / but bargaining power.

LARISA: I see young men carrying Kalashnikovs, women no older than me with gelignite and metallic objects: nails, blades, pins... / strapped to their stomachs.

ALEX: This is a deathtrap. The theatre is surrounded by military, all armed, all pointed at them. At us. These people will not get out alive, I see that now.

And if *they* can't, what hope is there for us?

Edwina Wren as Mother and Ryan Gibson as Boy in the 2007 Theatre@Risk
production. (Photo: Josephine Harkin)

RAISA: My husband and I were arguing because… the army want to station our son—in Grovzny. Chechnya. He's been told that, there, life is cheap. Some soldiers make money from locals who pay them *not* to torture their men. *Not* to rape their women.

They hate our people. Our people hate theirs. Here we are under one roof.

[*Sobbing*] He was only a child. I wanted to pick him up.

Pause.

LARISA: Saturday. October 26. Moscow. Five-forty-five a.m.

NIKOLAI: We are now sitting around a fifty-kilogram bomb.

ALEX: Plonked in the middle of the seats like a turd in a swimming pool. And we'd all love to swim as far away from it as we can. But we can't.

RAISA: The women are sitting in a circle around us with their fingers on the detonators. The men… I don't know where they are. But I know they're armed.

LARISA: I'm trying to move my feet because they keep going to sleep. I'm moving them slowly, carefully, under the seat. Because very soon now I think I need to be ready. To run.

NIKOLAI: Somehow they know, they suspect… the Russians are going to raid the theatre.

ALEX: The silence is killing me. And the fear. And we wait.

The hostages reach for each other, hold hands.

LARISA: Saturday. October 26. Moscow. Six-forty-five a.m. The beginning of the end. As we stare at the bomb in our midst, there is a strange sound.

NIKOLAI: A hissing sound, but it all happens so quickly…

Jingle of the shop bell.

ACTOR 3: Saturday. October 26. Newcastle. Six-forty-five p.m. He enters the bookshop for the last time.

ACTOR 1: And she, finishing her orders, looks up and gives him a smile.

BOOKSELLER: Is someone there? Can I help you, love?

YOUNG MAN: I'm just looking thanks.

BOOKSELLER: Don't rush, that's half the pleasure. [*As* ACTOR] And as she finishes writing…

RAISA: … in just a few seconds really, a strange smell like burning…

ALEX: … some of us aware that it must be gas but not all of us.

RAISA: … the auditorium fills with the strangest sound… [*almost laughing at the absurdity*] snoring…

ALEX: Most of the Chechens fall without even getting their gas masks open…

RAISA: … and all those fingers on all those detonators just… drop away.

BOOKSELLER: [*as* ACTOR] He comes over to the counter with two books in his hand. A young man in those baggy clothes. Thin. Pale. Awkward. [*To him, smiling*] Just in time. We close at seven.

YOUNG MAN: Yeah. Thanks for… waiting. Just these thanks. [*As* ACTOR] His hands are starting to shake and he's sweating like anything.

BOOKSELLER: Mmmm. This seems to be a very popular book with the young men. *Secrets of Western Sex Magic.*

The YOUNG MAN *shrugs, shuffles uneasily. She smiles a little.*

It's not a *dirty* book, you know.

YOUNG MAN: Yeah… I—

BOOKSELLER: No, it's more about Tantra. Delayed gratification, do you know about that?

YOUNG MAN: Not really, no.

She starts to write the title down on her list.

RAISA: There is something in the air, like a shimmer of heat, and my last thought is… I want to talk to my husband. Tell him I'm sorry. Because when we spoke before… I was so angry…

ALEX: I am shocked, confused, but I see it is also happening to the women with their knitting and the men with their guns and it occurs to me that whether I am falling asleep, or dying, they are experiencing the same thing. And I am glad.

JOURNALIST: Gas pours simultaneously into a room above, where some of the Chechen men are watching a video recording of their storming of the stage three nights ago. I presume their leader is among them.

REBEL LEADER: As we fall to the ground, Spetznaz soldiers burst through the roof and shoot us all. At the same time Alpha troops, hiding in a drain beneath the auditorium, enter and kill each of the unconscious Chechen women with a single shot to the temple.

JOURNALIST: And by seven o'clock the last shots have been fired and the first wave of hostage bodies are brought outside and dumped lifelessly on the carpark tarmac.

ALEX: It was like a lottery! *If* you were lucky enough to be carried with your head hanging forward, not backwards… to be placed in the recovery position… to be seen to by one of the few medics they had waiting… to be injected with the antidote… then maybe, maybe you'd survive.

JOURNALIST: One hundred and seventeen hostages, fifty Chechens dead.

ALEX: [*with a shrug*] The book was definitely better.

> *The* BOOKSELLER *and the* YOUNG MAN *take up their positions in the bookshop again.*

BOOKSELLER: So you read it and come back and tell me what you think. [*As* ACTOR] And she looks up…

YOUNG MAN: [*as* ACTOR] And she sees… between them, pointed at her face. [*As* YOUNG MAN, *to her, vicious*] Give me the money.

BOOKSELLER: Is that a gun?

YOUNG MAN: What do you think? Here… Bag, where is it? Here. Here! Fill it up. Fill it up!

BOOKSELLER: Why are you doing this?

YOUNG MAN: You *know* why I'm doing this. I want the money.

> *She hesitates, draws on inner reserves. She's scared but he seems vulnerable.*

BOOKSELLER: I can't, love.

> *He didn't expect that.*

YOUNG MAN: Yes you can.

BOOKSELLER: That money, it doesn't belong to me.

YOUNG MAN: You… just have to open it up and put it in.

BOOKSELLER: It's not my shop. I only work here. I'm sorry, love.

YOUNG MAN: [*furious*] I've got a gun! A shotgun! Do you know what this could do to you?

BOOKSELLER: What do you need the money for?

YOUNG MAN: Food—I need a feed. Alright?

BOOKSELLER: You're hungry?

YOUNG MAN: Yeah yeah, so… can you just put the money in the bag. [*Pause.*] Please?

BOOKSELLER: I've got some food. A bag of bread rolls. Some bananas. You can have those, you don't have to worry about *taking* them. / I'll *give* them to you.

YOUNG MAN: Swallow, try to focus… / Suddenly so tired…

BOOKSELLER: Bread rolls—you can *have* those…

YOUNG MAN: … not really up to this, sweating and / cold and try again.

BOOKSELLER: Bananas—I'll give them to you…

YOUNG MAN: The money!

BOOKSELLER: Have you got somewhere to sleep?

YOUNG MAN: What?

BOOKSELLER: Do you know about the refuge up the road? It's very good, very clean.

YOUNG MAN: I just… step back. Just step back. Losing. Gun dropping. Why is she being / so…

BOOKSELLER: Do you want me to call them, love? Or call yourself, you can use / this phone.

YOUNG MAN: … so fucking nice…

BOOKSELLER: Because I feel / sorry.

YOUNG MAN: … to me?

BOOKSELLER: Can I help you, love?

YOUNG MAN: He wipes at his face. Tired. Defeated. Gun seems too heavy. Shoulders sore.

BOOKSELLER: Let me help you. Please.

YOUNG MAN: No! [*Pause. Trying to do something*] I'm taking this. [*He grabs a book.*] And this. *Secrets of Western Sex Magic.*

BOOKSELLER: Take it. [*As* ACTOR] He gains some energy. Some spirit. Goes to leave and…

> *He snaps, turns on her. It's a plea but made with such anger, such violence.*

YOUNG MAN: You want to know what I want? I want *this*. I want to know the *secrets*. She hates me. We made a baby but she hates me now. So what's the fucking *secret*? I take drugs. I live on a mate's floor. I do two break-and-enters a fortnight just so I can walk on the street and hold my head up. I walk past people with their arms full of… food and cigarettes and all the things I can't buy, I have to steal to walk on the same street as them. They're looking at me, like I'm a piece of shit. Because of the secrets I don't know.

I don't know if they never got given me or if I'm just not allowed to know.

Sex. Food. House. The little things.

But they're not mine to have. Why?

> *The* BOOKSELLER *stares at him. Shock. As if she's been hit.*

ACTOR 1: Stuffs the gun back beneath his jacket, looks out to see if anyone is coming.

ACTOR 3: Grabs his plastic bag and pushes it back in his pocket,

YOUNG MAN: Holding the books, backs out of the shop, watching her watching him. Runs.

JOURNALIST: In the theatre, I saw only one hostage. A young woman in a yellow blouse. A rebel took her past me. My first thought was: God, please don't let him have raped her.

Because… I didn't want them to do this… in a dirty way.

But it may well have happened.

> *Pause.*

Any allegiance you may think you have—in your mind, can only be… to those who are suffering.

BOOKSELLER: The bell on the door rings as he runs out and in towards the shopping centre. I go to the door. Lock it. Turn the sign over.

She watches him go. The shock increases, gradually.

ACTOR 1: Walks out and back to the toilet; changes his shirt / puts a new one over the top.

YOUNG MAN: [*starting to swagger*] They'll catch me on the security camera later on. / Put the picture in the paper.

ACTOR 1: Heads to his mate's house and swaps gun for drugs. This gun's already been traded over and over from person to person. Next time it may turn up in a murder.

YOUNG MAN: [*swaggering*] Robber is offered a banana but settles for two books! Hey, mate! / See me in the paper?

ACTOR 1: Stay up for a couple of hours, maybe till next morning. Tell the whole story. Embellish. / Tell it again.

YOUNG MAN: Yeah, that's me! / That's me who done that bookshop. Seen me picture?

ACTOR 1: Use some of the drugs in cycles of a couple of days. Probably speed.

Go home. Adrenaline wears off.

YOUNG MAN: [*like the first scene—powerless*] Yeah… can I speak to Kelly please? Please? Oh right. / Yeah okay. Could you tell her I called? I just want to know how she's going. Can you tell her… I miss her? And… Luke? Thanks.

ACTOR 1: By day three he's back into his routine.

And he has to do this once or twice every fortnight. Job like this. Small job. Bookshop.

7-Eleven. / Break-and-enter.

The YOUNG MAN *registers. It's his life. And it's fucked.*

YOUNG MAN: Once or twice a fortnight. Job like this.

Pause.

ACTOR 3: Monday. October 28. Newcastle. Six-forty-five p.m.

The BOOKSELLER *trying to go on as normal. Nervous. Anxious. No more uninterrupted sleeps for a very long time.*

BOOKSELLER: [*taking a breath*] *Women Who Run with the Wolves*; *Chicken Soup for the Soul*; *A Cave in the Snow… Secrets of Western Sex Magic*. [*She stops. Grips her pen. Looks up—has she heard something? She is terrified and at breaking point.*]

Puts her pen down.

Steps up to the door, locks it.

Closed sign.

    Long pause—a whisper.

Lights off.

THE END

Visit our website to:

- Buy your books online
- Browse through our full list of titles, from plays to screenplays, books on theatre, film and music, and more
- Choose a play for your school or amateur performance group by cast size and gender
- Obtain information about performance rights
- Find out about theatre productions and other performing arts news across Australia
- For students, read our study guides
- For teachers, access syllabus and other relevant information
- Sign up for our email newsletter

The performing arts publisher

.

www.ingramcontent.com/pod-product-compliance
Lightning Source LLC
Chambersburg PA
CBHW041935090426
42744CB00017B/2065